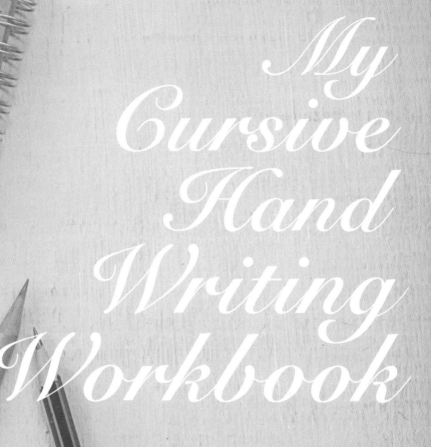

My Cursive Hand Writing Workbook

나만의
영어 필기체
연습장

넥서스콘텐츠개발팀 지음

넥서스

My Cursive Handwriting Workbook
나만의 영어 필기체 연습장

지은이 넥서스콘텐츠개발팀
펴낸이 임상진
펴낸곳 (주)넥서스

초판 1쇄 발행 2016년 12월 5일
초판 25쇄 발행 2022년 12월 23일

2판 1쇄 발행 2024년 2월 8일
2판 2쇄 발행 2024년 2월 15일

출판신고 1992년 4월 3일 제311-2002-2호
주소 10880 경기도 파주시 지목로 5
전화 (02)330-5500 팩스 (02)330-5555

ISBN 979-11-6683-768-5 13740

www.nexusbook.com

이 책의 특징

- 나만의 필기체로 멋진 문장을 쓸 수 있습니다.
- 카드, 편지, 캘리그래피 등에 쓰면 정말 멋집니다.
- 집중해서 쓰다 보면 저절로 스트레스가 풀립니다.
- 나만의 시간을 가지고 싶은 날, 이 책을 써 보세요.
- 명문, 유명 문구들을 쓰다 보면 영어 공부에도 도움이 됩니다.
- QR코드를 스캔하여 쓰기 동영상을 함께 보며 써 보세요.

이 책 사용법

- 펜을 엄지와 검지로 가볍게 잡고 중지로 받칩니다.
- 펜을 너무 짧게 잡거나 세워서 잡지는 마세요.
- 손과 손목의 긴장을 풀고 힘을 살짝 뺍니다.
- 차분하게 천천히 글자 모양을 따라 씁니다.
- 쓰는 법이 헷갈릴 때는 동영상을 참고하세요.

쓰기 동영상 보는 법

스마트폰에 QR코드 리더기를
설치하여 책 속의 QR코드를
스캔하세요!

Contents
차 례

Writing Warming Up

 ## Week 1

 ## Week 2

나만의 **영어 필기체 연습장**

Writing Warming Up

◀ 동영상 바로가기

Capital Letters

필기체 대문자

$\mathcal{A}$

A

$\mathcal{B}$

B

$\mathcal{C}$

C

$\mathcal{D}$

D

$\mathcal{E}$

E

$\mathcal{F}$

F

$\mathcal{G}$

G

$\mathcal{H}$

H

$\mathcal{I}$

I

$\mathcal{J}$

J

$\mathcal{K}$

K

$\mathcal{L}$

L

$\mathcal{M}$

M

$\mathcal{N}$

N

$\mathcal{O}$

O

$\mathcal{P}$

P

$\mathcal{Q}$

Q

$\mathcal{R}$

R

$\mathcal{S}$

S

$\mathcal{T}$

T

$\mathcal{U}$

U

$\mathcal{V}$

V

$\mathcal{W}$

W

$\mathcal{X}$

X

$\mathcal{Y}$

Y

$\mathcal{Z}$

Z

Small Letters

필기체 소문자

a

b

c

d

e

f

g

h

i

j

k

l

m

n

o

p

q

r

s

t

u

v

w

x

y

z

Writing Alphabet

A A A
a a a

ag와 ar을 써보세요.

ag ag ag
ar ar ar

B B B
b b b

be와 by를 써보세요.

be be be
by by by

C C C
c c c

ca와 ch를 써보세요.

ca ca ca
ch ch ch

D D D
d d d

de와 do를 써보세요.

de de de
do do do

E E E
e e e

ed와 ev를 써보세요.

ed ed ed
ev ev ev

F f

$\mathcal{F}\ \mathcal{F}\ \mathcal{F}$

$f\ f\ f$

fa와 fr을 써보세요.

fa fa fa

fr fr fr

G g

$\mathcal{G}\ \mathcal{G}\ \mathcal{G}$

$g\ g\ g$

ga와 gr을 써보세요.

ga ga ga

gr gr gr

H h

$\mathcal{H}\ \mathcal{H}\ \mathcal{H}$

$h\ h\ h$

ho와 hy를 써보세요.

ho ho ho

hy hy hy

I i

$\mathcal{I}\ \mathcal{I}\ \mathcal{I}$

$i\ i\ i$

il과 in을 써보세요.

il il il

in in in

J j

$\mathcal{J}\ \mathcal{J}\ \mathcal{J}$

$j\ j\ j$

je와 jo를 써보세요.

je je je

jo jo jo

Writing Alphabet

K K K

k k k

ke와 ky를 써보세요.

ke ke ke

ky ky ky

L L L

l l l

la와 lu를 써보세요.

la la la

lu lu lu

M M M

m m m

mo와 mu를 써보세요.

mo mo mo

mu mu mu

N N N

n n n

ne와 ny를 써보세요.

ne ne ne

ny ny ny

O O O

o o o

on과 oo를 써보세요.

on on on

oo oo oo

P p

P p

P P P

p p p

pa와 pr을 써보세요.

pa pa pa

pr pr pr

Q q

Q q

Q Q Q

q q q

qu와 qi를 써보세요.

qu qu qu

qi qi qi

R r

R r

R R R

r r r

rr과 ry를 써보세요.

rr rr rr

ry ry ry

S s

S s

S S S

s s s

se와 so를 써보세요.

se se se

so so so

T t

T t

T T T

t t t

th와 to를 써보세요.

th th th

to to to

Writing Alphabet

U u

U U U

u u u

un과 us를 써보세요.

un un un

us us us

V v

V V V

v v v

vi와 vy를 써보세요.

vi vi vi

vy vy vy

W w

W W W

w w w

wa와 wh를 써보세요.

wa wa wa

wh wh wh

X x

X X X

x x x

xe와 xy를 써보세요.

xe xe xe

xy xy xy

Y y

Y Y Y

y y y

ye와 yo를 써보세요.

ye ye ye

yo yo yo

ze와 zo를 써보세요.

Z z

Z Z Z *ze ze ze*

Z Z Z *zo zo zo*

대문자 이어써보기

$ABCDEFGHIJKLMNOPQRSTUVWXYZ$

소문자 이어써보기

$abcdefghijklmnopqrstuvwxyz$

15

나만의 **영어 필기체 연습장**

Week 1

◀ 동영상 바로가기

Daily

Dear,
친애하는 ~에게
(편지나 메일을 시작할 때 써요)

Dear,

See you soon!
곧 만나!

See you soon!

Sincerely yours,
당신의 진실한 벗 ~으로부터
(편지나 메일 끝에 써요)

Sincerely yours,

What a surprise!
놀라워!

What a surprise!

Long time no see!
오랜만이야

Long time no see!

How are you today?
오늘 어때?

How are you today?

Thank you very much!
정말 고마워!

Thank you very much!

I hope everything is okay.
별일 없었으면 좋겠어.

I hope everything is okay.

Daily

Me too.
나도 그래.

Me too.

It's great!
멋지다!

It's great!

Good luck.
행운을 빌어.

Good luck.

take a note
노트하기

take a note

Are you sure?

정말?

Are you sure?

Congratulations!

축하해!

Congratulations!

That's a great idea.

좋은 생각이야.

That's a great idea.

Sorry. It was all my fault.

미안해. 다 내 잘못이야.

Sorry. It was all my fault.

I love you.

사랑해.

> I love you.

LIVE,
LAUGH,
LOVE

삶, 웃음, 사랑

> LIVE, LAUGH, LOVE

All you
need is love.

당신에게 필요한 건 사랑이에요.
– 비틀즈 –

> All you need is love.

Don't forget
to love yourself.

자신을 사랑하는 것을 잊지 말아요.

> Don't forget to love yourself.

If you wished to be loved, love.

사랑받길 원한다면 사랑하세요.

If you wished to be loved, love.

Where there is love, there is life.

사랑이 있는 곳에 삶이 있다.
- 간디 -

Where there is love, there is life.

Who, being loved, is poor?

사랑을 받는 어떤 자가 불행한가요?
- 오스카 와일드 -

Who, being loved, is poor?

Bitterness imprisons life; love releases it.

괴로움은 삶을 구속하지만,
사랑은 그것을 해방시킨다.

Bitterness imprisons life; love releases it.

Romance

Romance is everything.

로맨스는 모든 것의 전부이다.

Romance is everything.

Beauty is the lover's gift.

아름다움은 사랑하는 사람의 선물이다.
– 작가 윌리엄 콩그리브 –

Beauty is the lover's gift.

Romantic love is an addiction.

낭만적 사랑은 일종의 중독이다.

Romantic love is an addiction.

My heart is like a singing bird.

내 마음은 노래하는 새와 같아요.
– 시인 크리스티나 로제티 –

My heart is like a singing bird.

**True love
stories never
have endings.**

진실한 사랑은 절대로
끝나지 않는다.
- 소설가 리처드 바크 -

True love stories never have endings.

**You are the
source
of my joy.**

당신은 내가 즐거운 이유입니다.

You are the source of my joy.

**You came
and changed
my world.**

당신은 내게 와서
내 세상을 바꾸었다.

You came and changed my world.

**I don't need
paradise because
I found you.**

당신을 찾은 나는
천국이 필요 없어요.

I don't need paradise because I found you.

Family

I love my family.
우리 가족을 사랑해요.

I love my family.

Family is my everything.
가족은 내 모든 것입니다.

Family is my everything.

Home is where the heart is.
집은 사랑하는
사람들이 있는 곳이다.

Home is where the heart is.

Family is a gift that lasts forever.
가족은 영원히 지속되는 선물이다.

Family is a gift that lasts forever.

Family is life's greatest blessing.

가족은 인생 최대의 축복이다.

Family is life's greatest blessing.

A good home must be made not bought.

좋은 가정이란 사는 것이 아니라 만들어지는 것이다.
– 소설가 조이스 메이나드 –

A good home must be made not bought.

There's no place like home.

집만 한 곳이 없다.

There's no place like home.

A happy family is but an earlier heaven.

행복한 가정은 지상의 천국이다.
– 버나드 쇼 –

A happy family is but an earlier heaven.

27

Friendship

Best Friends Forever!
친구여 영원하라!

Best Friends Forever!

Friends are born, not made.
친구는 타고나는 것이지,
만들어지는 것이 아니다.
– 소설가 헨리 애덤스 –

Friends are born, not made.

Good friends are hard to find.
좋은 친구는 찾기 어렵다.

Good friends are hard to find.

Friends are the sunshine of life.
친구는 인생의 햇살이다.

Friends are the sunshine of life.

Time makes friendship stronger.

시간은 우정을 강하게 한다.

Time makes friendship stronger.

A friend is a gift you give yourself.

친구란 당신에게 주는 선물이다.

A friend is a gift you give yourself.

A friend in need is a friend indeed.

어려울 때 친구가 진정한 친구이다.

A friend in need is a friend indeed.

A friend is a second self.

친구란 제2의 자신이다.
- 아리스토텔레스 -

A friend is a second self.

Beauty

You
are beautiful.

당신은 아름다워요.

You are beautiful.

Beauty is
not in the face.

아름다움은 얼굴에 있는 것이 아니다.

Beauty is not in the face.

Things are
beautiful if you
love them.

사랑하면 그 대상은 아름답게 보인다.
- 프랑스 극작가 장 아누이 -

Things are beautiful if you love them.

True beauty
comes from
within.

진정한 아름다움은 내면에서 온다.

True beauty comes from within.

Beauty awakens the soul to act.

아름다움은 영혼을 움직이게 한다.
– 이탈리아 시인 단테 알리기에리 –

Beauty awakens the soul to act.

Beauty is in the eye of the beholder.

아름다움이란 보는 사람의
눈에 달린 것이다.

Beauty is in the eye of the beholder.

Beauty is a light in the heart.

아름다움은
마음에 있는 빛이다.

Beauty is a light in the heart.

There is a kind of beauty in imperfection.

완벽하지 않은 것에도
아름다움은 존재한다.

There is a kind of beauty in imperfection.

31

Dream

I am a dreamer.
나는 꿈꾸는 사람입니다.

I am a dreamer.

You can plant a dream.
당신은 꿈을 심을 수 있어요.
– 앤 캠벨 –

You can plant a dream.

Follow your dreams.
당신의 꿈을 따르세요.

Follow your dreams.

Dream it, Wish it, Do it
꿈꾸라, 원하라, 행동하라

Dream it, Wish it, Do it

Make your dreams happen.

당신의 꿈이
이루어지도록 해보세요.

Make your dreams happen.

Dream as if you'll live forever.

영원히 살 것처럼 꿈꾸라.

Dream as if you'll live forever.

Sometimes your dreams come true.

때때로 당신의 꿈이 이루어집니다.
- 복서 프랭크 브루노 -

Sometimes your dreams come true.

Nothing happens unless first we dream.

꿈꾸기 전에는 어떤 일도
일어나지 않는다.

Nothing happens unless first we dream.

Diet

Stay Healthy
건강하기

Stay Healthy

Let's lose weight!
같이 살 빼요!

Let's lose weight!

You earn your body.
당신의 몸은 당신이 만드는 것이다.

You earn your body.

The first wealth is health.
건강이 최고의 자산이다.
- 시인 랄프 왈도 에머슨 -

The first wealth is health.

Happiness lies first of all in health.

행복은 무엇보다 건강에 있다.

Happiness lies first of all in health.

A feeble body weakens the mind.

허약한 육체는 정신을 나약하게 한다.
- 장자크 루소 -

A feeble body weakens the mind.

---

change your mind & change your body

마음을 바꾸고 몸을 변화시키자

change your mind & change your body

Your body is a reflection of your lifestyle.

몸은 당신의
생활방식을 보여준다.

Your body is a reflection of your lifestyle.

Anniversary

Wishing you a Happy New Year!

새해 복 많이 받아요!

Wishing you a Happy New Year!

Happy Valentine's Day!

해피 밸런타인데이!

Happy Valentine's Day!

We wish you a merry Christmas!

메리 크리스마스!

We wish you a merry Christmas!

We wish you a very Happy holidays.

행복한 휴일 보내세요.

We wish you a very Happy holidays.

May you have a spectacular New Year.

멋진 새해를
맞이하시길 바랍니다.

May you have a spectacular New Year.

Merry christmas to your family!

당신 가족에게
메리 크리스마스!

Merry christmas to your family!

Warmest greetings and best wishes.

원하는 모든 일들이
이루어지길 바랍니다.

Warmest greetings and best wishes.

Happy Birthday to you!

생일 축하해!

Happy Birthday to you!

나만의 영어 필기체 연습장

Week 2

공부 *Study*

일 *Work*

비즈니스 *Business*

성공 *Success*

실패 *Failure*

태도 *Attitude*

리더십 *Leadership*

지식 *Knowledge*

실수 *Mistake*

기회 *Chance*

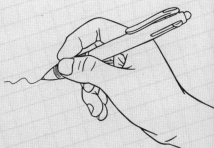

◀ 동영상 바로가기

Study

Do your best.
최선을 다하세요.

Do your best.

Education is the best provision for old age.
교육은 노후를 위한 최상의 양식이다.
- 아리스토텔레스 -

Education is the best provision for old age.

Wake up, seize the day.
일어나서, 기회를 잡으세요.

Wake up, seize the day.

Study while others are sleeping.
다른 사람들이 잘 때 공부하라.

Study while others are sleeping.

Study hard now and enjoy later.

지금 열심히 공부하고, 나중에 즐기자.

Study hard now and enjoy later.

Nothing worth having comes easy.

값진 것은 쉽게 얻을 수 없다.

Nothing worth having comes easy.

KEEP CALM AND DESTROY EXAMS.

침착하자, 시험을 끝장내자.

KEEP CALM AND DESTROY EXAMS.

To acquire knowledge, one must study.

지식을 얻으려면 공부를 해야 한다.
- 칼럼니스트 마릴린 사반트 -

To acquire knowledge, one must study.

Work

Love
what you do.

자신이 하는 일을 사랑하세요

| Love what you do.

Work hard,
dream big.

열심히 일하고, 꿈을 크게 꿔라.

| Work hard, dream big.

Hard work
beats talent.

꾸준한 노력만이
재능을 앞설 수 있다.

| Hard work beats talent.

There is no
substitute for
hard work.

노력을 대신할 수 있는 것은
아무것도 없다.
- 에디슨 -

| There is no substitute for hard work.

Without labor nothing prospers.

노동이 없이는
어떤 것도 자라지 않는다.
- 소포클레스 -

Without labor nothing prospers.

Hard work always pays off.

공들인 일은 결실을 맺는다.

Hard work always pays off.

A job isn't just a job. It's who you are.

직업은 당신이
누구인가를 나타낸다.

A job isn't just a job. It's who you are.

Don't complain. Just work harder.

불평하지 말고,
더 열심히 일하라.

Don't complain. Just work harder.

Business

Exchange ideas frequently.

아이디어를 자주 교환하라.
– 사업가 제임스 캐시 페니 –

Exchange ideas frequently.

Test fast, fail fast, adjust fast.

빨리 시험하고, 빨리 실패하고,
빨리 조정하라.
– 경영학자 톰 피터스 –

Test fast, fail fast, adjust fast.

Details create the big picture.

작은 것들이 모여
큰 그림을 만든다.

Details create the big picture.

So little done, so much to do.

한 것은 너무 없는데,
해야 할 일은 너무 많다.
– 정치가 세실 로즈 –

So little done, so much to do.

If it doesn't sell, it isn't creative.

팔리지 않는다면,
그건 창의적인 게 아니다.

If it doesn't sell, it isn't creative.

Punctuality is the soul of business.

시간 엄수는 비즈니스의 영혼이다.
- 토마스 할리버튼 -

Punctuality is the soul of business.

Word of mouth is the best medium of all.

말은 가장 좋은 수단이다.
- 크리에이터 윌리엄 번벅 -

Word of mouth is the best medium of all.

We're all working together.

우리는 함께 일한다.

We're all working together.

Success

Be brave and take risks.
용감하라,
그리고 위험을 감수하라.

Be brave and take risks.

Success comes with hard work.
성공은 열심히 일한 후 따라온다.

Success comes with hard work.

Success is dependent on effort.
성공은 노력에 달려 있다.

Success is dependent on effort.

Action is the key to all success.
성공의 모든 열쇠는
행동하는 것이다.
- 피카소 -

Action is the key to all success.

There is no success without hardship.

고난 없이는 성공도 없다.
– 소포클레스 –

There is no success without hardship.

There is no elevator to success.

성공에는 지름길이 없다.

There is no elevator to success.

You must believe that you can.

(성공하기 위해서는) 당신이
할 수 있다고 믿어야 한다.

You must believe that you can.

Winning is the only thing.

이기는 것이 유일한 것이다.

Winning is the only thing.

Failure

Don't be afraid of failure.

실패를 두려워하지 마세요.

Don't be afraid of failure.

Failing is not always failure.

실패하는 것이
항상 실패인 것은 아니다.

Failing is not always failure.

Try and fail, but never fail to try.

시도는 실패할 수 있지만
시도하는 것은 실패하지 마라.

Try and fail, but never fail to try.

Every failure is a step to success.

모든 실패는 성공으로
향하는 디딤돌이다.
- 윌리엄 휴얼 -

Every failure is a step to success.

Fall seven times, stand up eight.

일곱 번 넘어지면
여덟 번째 일어나라.

Fall seven times, stand up eight.

Sometimes the best gain is to lose.

가끔은 잃는 것이
최고의 기회가 될 수 있다.
- 조지 허버트 -

Sometimes the best gain is to lose.

There is no failure except giving up.

포기하는 것 외에는 실패란 없다.

There is no failure except giving up.

No man is a failure who is enjoying life.

삶을 즐긴다면
인간에게 실패란 없다.
- 윌리엄 페더 -

No man is a failure who is enjoying life.

Attitude

Respect differences.

차이를 존중하세요.

Respect differences.

You get what you give.

뿌린 대로 거둔다.

You get what you give.

Brevity is the soul of wit.

간결함은 지혜의 본질이다.
– 셰익스피어 –

Brevity is the soul of wit.

Honesty is the best policy.

정직이 최상의 방책이다.
– 벤자민 프랭클린 –

Honesty is the best policy.

Everybody needs somebody.

모두가 누군가를 필요로 해요.

Everybody needs somebody.

Don't be afraid to ask for help.

도움을 요청하는 걸
두려워 마세요.

Don't be afraid to ask for help.

Attitude determines the altitude of life.

태도가 삶의 고도를 결정한다.
- 에드윈 루이스 콜 -

Attitude determines the altitude of life.

The only disability in life is a bad attitude.

삶의 유일한 장애물은 나쁜 태도이다.

The only disability in life is a bad attitude.

Leadership

Example is leadership.

모범이 리더십이다.
- 알버트 슈바이처 -

Example is leadership.

Leadership is influence.

리더십은 영향력이다.
- 존 맥스웰 -

Leadership is influence.

A leader is a dealer in hope.

지도자는 희망을 파는 상인이다.
- 나폴레옹 -

A leader is a dealer in hope.

Don't find fault, find a remedy.

잘못된 점을 찾지 말고,
해결책을 찾아라.
- 헨리 포드 -

Don't find fault, find a remedy.

What helps people, helps business.

사람들에게 좋은 것이라면
비즈니스에도 좋다.
- 레오 버넷 -

What helps people, helps business.

Today a reader, tomorrow a leader.

오늘 책을 읽는 자가
내일의 지도자이다.
- 마가렛 풀러 -

Today a reader, tomorrow a leader.

Leadership is being a servant first.

리더십은 먼저 섬기는 자가
되어 보는 것이다.

Leadership is being a servant first.

Leadership doesn't depend on being right.

리더십은 옳고 그름에
달려 있는 것이 아니다.

Leadership doesn't depend on being right.

Knowledge

Knowledge is power.
아는 것이 힘이다.

Knowledge is power.

Knowledge empowers you.
지식은 당신에게 힘을 부여한다.

Knowledge empowers you.

Always seek knowledge.
항상 지식을 추구하라.

Always seek knowledge.

The adventure of life is to learn.
인생의 모험은 배우는 것이다.

The adventure of life is to learn.

Learning never exhaust the mind.

학문은 결코 정신을
지치게 하지 않는다.
– 레오나르도 다 빈치 –

Learning never exhaust the mind.

All of life is a constant education.

인생은 끊임없는 교육이다.

All of life is a constant education.

Power is gained by sharing knowledge.

힘은 지식을 나누는 것을
통해 생긴다.

Power is gained by sharing knowledge.

A good decision is based on knowledge.

좋은 결정은 지식에 근거한다.
– 플라톤 –

A good decision is based on knowledge.

Mistake

We all make mistakes.

우리는 모두 실수를 한다.

We all make mistakes.

The biggest mistake is complacency.

가장 큰 실수는 안주하는 것이다.
– 기업인 보니 해머 –

The biggest mistake is complacency.

Your best teacher is your last mistake.

가장 좋은 선생님은
당신의 마지막 실수이다.
– 시민운동가 랠프 네이더 –

Your best teacher is your last mistake.

Life is not life unless you make mistakes.

실수를 하지 않는 삶은
삶이 아니다.

Life is not life unless you make mistakes.

Making mistakes is a part of life.

실수하는 것은
인생의 한 부분이다.

Making mistakes is a part of life.

We learn from failure, not from success.

우리는 성공이 아니라,
실패를 통해 배운다.

We learn from failure, not from success.

Wise men learn by other men's mistakes.

현명한 사람은
다른 사람의 실수를 통해 배운다.

Wise men learn by other men's mistakes.

Mistakes are proof that you are trying.

실수는 당신이 노력하고
있다는 증거이다.

Mistakes are proof that you are trying.

Chance

Take a chance!

기회를 놓치지 마라!

Take a chance!

Everyday is a second chance.

매일은 우리에게 주어지는
두 번째 기회이다.

Everyday is a second chance.

If you never try, you'll never know.

시도하지 않는다면,
영원히 모를 것이다

If you never try, you'll never know.

Always do what you are afraid to do.

두려운 일은 반드시 해라.
- 시인 랄프 왈도 에머슨 -

Always do what you are afraid to do.

The only safe thing is to take a chance.

가장 안전한 것은 기회를 잡는 것이다.
– 영화감독 마이크 니콜스 –

The only safe thing is to take a chance.

Just keep taking chances.

기회를 잡고 즐겨라.

Just keep taking chances.

To success, one must take chances.

성공하기 위해서는
기회를 잡아야 한다.

To success, one must take chances.

If the sun comes up, I have a chance.

해가 떠오른다면,
나에게 기회가 있다는 것이다.

If the sun comes up, I have a chance.

나만의 **영어 필기체 연습장**

Week 3

나이 Age
인생 Life
경험 Experience
지혜 Wisdom
변화 Change
미래 Future
시간 Time
여행 Travel
영화 명대사 Movie
노래 가사 Music

▶ 동영상 바로가기

Age

Age is no barrier.

나이는 장애물이 아니다.

Age is no barrier.

Youth has no age.

젊음에는 나이가 없다.
– 피카소 –

Youth has no age.

If youth knew; if age could.

젊음은 알지 못한 것을 탄식하고,
나이는 하지 못한 것을 탄식한다.
– 프로이트 –

If youth knew; if age could.

Age is no guarantee of maturity.

나이가 성숙함을
보장하지는 않는다.

Age is no guarantee of maturity.

Live your life and forget your age!

자신의 나이를 잊고
자기만의 삶을 살아라!

Live your life and forget your age!

Minds ripen at very different ages.

마음은 각자 다른 나이에 무르익는다.
- 스티비 원더 -

Minds ripen at very different ages.

Age is a matter of feeling.

나이는 (햇수의 문제가 아니라)
기분의 문제이다.

Age is a matter of feeling.

Every age has its happiness and troubles.

모든 나이마다
각각의 행복과 문제가 있다.
- 잔 칼망 -

Every age has its happiness and troubles.

So it goes.

그렇게 흘러가겠지.

So it goes.

Life is short.

인생은 짧아요.

Life is short.

Life is beautiful.

인생은 아름다워요.

Life is beautiful.

Life is the most wonderful fairy tale.

인생은 그 자체로
아름다운 동화이다.
– 한스 안데르센 –

Life is the most wonderful fairy tale.

Live each day as if it's your last.

매일이 마지막인 것처럼 살라.

Live each day as if it's your last.

If you love life, don't waste time.

삶을 사랑한다면,
시간을 낭비하지 말라.
- 브루스 리 -

If you love life, don't waste time.

Our life is what our thoughts make it.

우리의 인생은
우리의 생각들이 결정한다.
- 마르쿠스 아우렐리우스 -

Our life is what our thoughts make it.

Life is about creating yourself.

인생은 당신을
만들어가는 것이다.

Life is about creating yourself.

Experience

Experience is a great teacher.

경험은 위대한 스승이다.

Experience is a great teacher.

Every moment is an experience.

모든 순간이 경험이다.
- 프로레슬러 제이크 로버츠 -

Every moment is an experience.

Stay patient and trust your journey.

침착하게 당신의
여정을 믿어 보세요.

Stay patient and trust your journey.

Nothing can substitute experience.

경험을 대신할 것은 아무것도 없다.
- 파울로 코엘료 -

Nothing can substitute experience.

The reward of suffering is experience.

고통의 보상은 경험이다.
– 헤리 트루먼 –

The reward of suffering is experience.

Experience is the teacher of all things.

경험은 모든 것의 스승이다.

Experience is the teacher of all things.

We are a product of all our experiences.

우리는 경험의 산물이다.

We are a product of all our experiences.

The source of knowledge is experience.

지식의 원천은 경험이다.
– 아인슈타인 –

The source of knowledge is experience.

Wisdom

Wisdom begins in wonder.

지혜는 호기심에서 시작한다.
- 소크라테스 -

Wisdom begins in wonder.

Wisdom outweighs any wealth.

지혜는 그 어떤 재산보다
중요하다.

Wisdom outweighs any wealth.

Turn your wounds into wisdom.

당신의 상처를 지혜로 만드세요.
- 오프라 윈프리 -

Turn your wounds into wisdom.

Wisdom is knowing what to do next.

지혜란 다음에 할 일이
무엇인지 아는 것이다.

Wisdom is knowing what to do next.

A wise man makes his own decisions.

현명한 사람은 <u>스스로</u> 결정한다.

A wise man makes his own decisions.

Wisdom is the right use of knowledge.

지혜는 지식의 올바른 사용이다.

Wisdom is the right use of knowledge.

Knowledge speaks, but wisdom listens.

지식은 말을 하지만, 지혜는 듣는다.
– 지미 헨드릭스 –

Knowledge speaks, but wisdom listens.

Wisdom sails with wind and time.

지혜는 바람, 시간과 함께
항해한다.
– 존 플로리오 –

Wisdom sails with wind and time.

Change

Change the world!
세상을 바꿔라!

Change the world!

Change is inevitable.
변화는 불가피하다.

Change is inevitable.

Only I can change my life.
오직 나만이 내 인생을 바꿀 수 있다.

Only I can change my life.

Change brings opportunity.
변화는 기회를 가져온다.
– 니도 쿠베인 –

Change brings opportunity.

Change before you have to.

변화가 필요하기 전에 변하라.
– 잭 웰치 –

Change before you have to.

Nothing endures but change.

변화 외에 불변하는 것은 없다.
– 헤라클레이토스 –

Nothing endures but change.

Things do not change; we change.

세상은 변하지 않는다.
우리가 변한다.

Things do not change; we change.

Ignorance is always afraid of change.

무지함은 항상 변화를 두려워한다.
– 자와할랄 네루 –

Ignorance is always afraid of change.

Future

The future is now.

미래는 지금 이 순간이다.

The future is now.

Your future is bright.

당신의 미래는 밝다.

Your future is bright.

Only you can control your future.

오직 당신만이
미래를 통제할 수 있다.
– 작가 닥터 수스 –

Only you can control your future.

The past doesn't equal the future.

과거는 미래와 같지 않다.

The past doesn't equal the future.

Your past never defines your future.

당신의 과거가 당신의 미래를 결정짓는 것은 아니다.

Your past never defines your future.

The youth is the hope of our future.

젊은이들이 우리 미래의 희망이다.
- 필리핀 영웅 호세 리잘 -

The youth is the hope of our future.

The future starts today, not tomorrow.

미래는 내일이 아닌 오늘 시작한다.
- 요한 바오로 2세 -

The future starts today, not tomorrow.

The best way to predict future is create it.

미래를 예측하는 가장 좋은 방법은 그것을 만드는 것이다.

The best way to predict future is create it.

Time

Time flies.

시간은 흘러간다.

Time flies.

Time is money.

시간은 돈이다.

Time is money.

Lost time is never found again.

잃어버린 시간은 다시 찾을 수 없다.
- 벤자민 프랭클린 -

Lost time is never found again.

We must use time creatively.

시간을 창조적으로 보내야 한다.

We must use time creatively.

**Time is free,
but it's priceless.**

시간은 무료지만 값을 따질 수 없다.

Time is free, but it's priceless.

**Time is flying
never to return.**

시간은 흐르고 두 번 다시
돌아오지 않는다.
- 베르질리우스 -

Time is flying never to return.

**There is no
time to waste.**

낭비할 시간이 없다.

There is no time to waste.

**You may
delay, but time
will not.**

당신은 지체할 수 있지만
시간은 그렇지 않다.

You may delay, but time will not.

Travel

See the world!
세상을 보래!

See the world!

Go on an adventure.
모험을 떠나요.

Go on an adventure.

I am a travel enthusiast.
나는 여행광이에요.

I am a travel enthusiast.

Wherever you go, go with all your heart.
어디를 가든 온 마음을 다해 가라.
- 공자 -

Wherever you go, go with all your heart.

Travel teaches as much as books.

여행은 책 못지않게
많은 것을 가르쳐준다.
− 세네갈 가수 유쑨두 −

Travel teaches as much as books.

Life is short and the world is wide.

인생은 짧고 세상은 넓다.

Life is short and the world is wide.

Travel far enough you meet yourself.

자신을 만날 만큼
멀리 여행하라.

Travel far enough you meet yourself.

The world is yours to explore.

세상은 탐험할 수 있는
당신의 것이에요.

The world is yours to explore.

Movie

**The heart wants
what it wants.**

마음은 그것이 원하는 것을 원해요.
〈노트북〉

The heart wants what it wants.

**You are the
reason I am.**

당신은 내가 존재하는 이유입니다.
〈뷰티풀 마인드〉

You are the reason I am.

**Life is a
box of
chocolates.**

인생이란 초콜릿 상자와 같아.
〈포레스트 검프〉

Life is a box of chocolates.

**May the Force
be with you.**

신이 당신과 함께 하기를.
〈스타워즈〉

May the Force be with you.

Manners makes man.

매너가 사람을 만든다.
〈킹스맨〉

Manners makes man.

Experience never gets old.

경험은 결코 늙지 않는다.
〈인턴〉

Experience never gets old.

Anyone can be anything.

누구나 무엇이든 될 수 있어요.
〈주토피아〉

Anyone can be anything.

Life isn't always what one like.

삶이란 언제나
뜻대로 되는 것이 아니에요.
〈로마의 휴일〉

Life isn't always what one like.

Music

You are not alone.

당신은 혼자가 아니에요.
〈You Are Not Alone, 마이클 잭슨〉

You are not alone.

Isn't she lovely?

그녀 정말 사랑스럽지 않나요?
〈Isn't She Lovely, 스티비 원더〉

Isn't she lovely?

I was born to love you.

나는 당신을 사랑하기 위해 태어났어요.
〈I Was Born To Love You, 퀸〉

I was born to love you.

A hero lies in you.

당신 안에 영웅이 있어요.
〈Hero, 머라이어 캐리〉

A hero lies in you.

Wanna love you in slow motion.

당신을 천천히 사랑하고 싶어요.
〈Slow Motion, 카리나〉

Wanna love you in slow motion.

There will be an answer. Let it be.

순리에 맡기세요.
그곳에 답이 있을 거예요.
〈Let It Be, 비틀즈〉

There will be an answer. Let it be.

You raise me up to more than I can be.

당신은 내가 될 수 있는 것보다
더 높게 일으켜줍니다.
〈You Raise Me Up, 웨스트라이프〉

You raise me up to more than I can be.

I don't know why I didn't come.

왜 내가 당신에게 가지 않았는지는
나도 모르겠어요.
〈Don't Know Why, 노라 존스〉

I don't know why I didn't come.

나만의 **영어 필기체 연습장**

Week 4

긍정 *Positiveness*
행복 *Happiness*
웃음 *Laughter*
감사 *Thanks*
행운 *Fortune*
믿음 *Faith*
영감 *Inspiration*
위로 *Comfort*
희망 *Hope*
평화 *Peace*

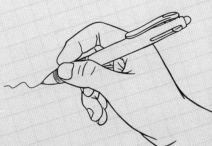

◀ 동영상 바로가기

Positiveness

Nothing is impossible.

불가능한 것은 없다.

Nothing is impossible.

Think positive, be positive!

긍정적으로 생각하고
긍정적인 사람 되기!

Think positive, be positive!

Positive thinking takes you far.

긍정적인 생각은 당신을
멀리 데려다줄 거예요.

Positive thinking takes you far.

Be positive and laugh at everything.

긍정적으로 생각하고
모든 것에 웃어요.
- 영화배우 알렉산드라 로치 -

Be positive and laugh at everything.

A positive attitude gives you power.

긍정적인 생각은
당신에게 힘을 줍니다.

A positive attitude gives you power.

A positive attitude changes everything.

긍정적인 태도가
모든 것을 변화시킨다.

A positive attitude changes everything.

I believe in being positive.

긍정을 믿어요.
- 미식축구 선수 조 그린 -

I believe in being positive.

the power of positive thinking

긍정의 힘

the power of positive thinking

Happiness

What makes you happy?

무엇이 당신을
행복하게 하나요?

| What makes you happy?

Be happy for this moment.

이 순간에 행복하라.

| Be happy for this moment.

Be happy & be bright & be you!

행복하기 & 밝아지기
& 나 자신 되기!

| Be happy & be bright & be you!

You can be happy where you are.

당신이 있는 곳에서
행복할 수 있습니다.
- 조엘 오스틴 -

| You can be happy where you are.

86

Happiness depends upon ourselves.

행복은 우리에게 달렸다.
- 아리스토텔레스 -

Happiness depends upon ourselves.

Today is the perfect day to be happy!

오늘은 행복하기
좋은 날이에요!

Today is the perfect day to be happy!

Happiness is itself a kind of gratitude.

행복은 바로
감사하는 마음입니다.

Happiness is itself a kind of gratitude.

The purpose of our lives is to be happy.

우리 삶의 목적은
행복해지기 위해서이다.
- 달라이 라마 -

The purpose of our lives is to be happy.

Laughter

Don't forget to smile!

웃는 거 잊지 말기!

Don't forget to smile!

Peace begins with a smile.

평화는 미소에서부터 시작한다
– 마더 테레사 –

Peace begins with a smile.

You have a cute smile, smile more!

당신의 웃음은 귀여워요,
계속 웃어요!

You have a cute smile, smile more!

Laughing is the best form of therapy.

최고의 치료법은 웃음이다.

Laughing is the best form of therapy.

A good laugh is sunshine in a house.

웃음은 집 안의 햇볕이다.
– 소설가 윌리엄 새커리 –

A good laugh is sunshine in a house.

Humor is mankind's greatest blessing.

유머는 인류의
가장 위대한 축복이다.

Humor is mankind's greatest blessing.

A day without laughter is a day wasted.

웃음 없는 하루는 낭비한 하루이다.
– 찰리 채플린 –

A day without laughter is a day wasted.

Smile while you still have teeth.

이가 남아 있을 때 많이 웃어라.

Smile while you still have teeth.

Thanks

Be thankful!
감사하라!

| Be thankful!

Gratitude is the sign of noble souls.
감사함은 귀귀한 마음의 표시이다.
– 이솝 –

| Gratitude is the sign of noble souls.

Be grateful for small things.
작은 일들에 감사하기

| Be grateful for small things.

Be thankful for the difficult times.
어려운 시기에
감사하는 마음 갖기

| Be thankful for the difficult times.

Start each day with a grateful heart.

감사하는 마음으로
매일매일을 시작하기

Start each day with a grateful heart.

You are blessed.

당신은 복받은 사람이에요.

You are blessed.

Appreciate everything that you have.

당신이 가진 모든 것에
감사하세요.

Appreciate everything that you have.

Unseasonable kindness gets no thanks.

적절하지 못한 친절함은
감사받지 못한다.
- 토마스 풀러 -

Unseasonable kindness gets no thanks.

Fortune

**I feel
very lucky.**

정말 행운이에요.

> I feel very lucky.

**making
my own luck**

나만의 행운 만들기

> making my own luck

**Everything
in life is luck.**

삶의 모든 것은 행운이다.
– 도널드 트럼프 –

> Everything in life is luck.

**Luck is
believing
you're lucky.**

행운은 당신이
운이 있다고 믿는 것이다.
– 테네시 윌리엄스 –

> Luck is believing you're lucky.

Care and diligence bring luck.

배려와 근면함은
행운을 가져온다.

Care and diligence bring luck.

Luck is being ready for the chance.

행운은 기회를 위한
준비를 하는 것이다.

Luck is being ready for the chance.

The champion makes his own luck.

챔피언은 스스로의 행운을 만든다.

The champion makes his own luck.

The harder I work, the luckier I get.

열심히 노력할수록,
행운은 더 다가온다.
- 영화 프로듀서 사무엘 골드윈 -

The harder I work, the luckier I get.

Faith

God only knows.

신만이 알고 있다.

God only knows.

I believe in god.

나는 신을 믿는다.

I believe in god.

God continues to work miracles.

신은 계속해서
기적을 만들어주신다.
- 영화배우 윌리 아메스 -

God continues to work miracles.

In him, there is no darkness at all.

그 안에서 어둠이란 없다.

In him, there is no darkness at all.

Worry ends when faith in god begins.

신에 대한 믿음이 시작될 때
걱정은 끝난다.

| Worry ends when faith in god begins.

Have faith in god; god has faith in you.

신에 대한 믿음을 가지면,
그도 당신에 믿음을 가질 것이다.
– 에드윈 루이스 콜 –

| Have faith in god; god has faith in you.

We walk by faith, not by sight.

보이지 않아도
믿음으로 걷는다.

| We walk by faith, not by sight.

Where god guides, he provides.

그가 이끄는 곳에서
베풀어주실 것이다.

| Where god guides, he provides.

Inspiration

Either move or be moved.

제거하거나 제거되거나
- 시인 에즈라 파운드 -

Either move or be moved.

When one must, one can.

꼭 해내야 할 때
우리는 그것을 할 수 있다.

When one must, one can.

Never, never, never give up!

절대로, 절대로, 절대로
포기하지 말기!

Never, never, never give up!

Well done is better than well said.

실천이 말보다 낫다.
- 벤자민 프랭클린 -

Well done is better than well said.

Never complain and never explain.

불평도 하지 말고 해명도 하지 말라.
- 정치가 벤자민 디즈레일리 -

Never complain and never explain.

If you can dream it, you can do it.

꿈꿀 수 있다면
그것을 해낼 수도 있다.
- 월트 디즈니 -

If you can dream it, you can do it.

Step by step and the thing is done.

한 걸음씩 나아가다 보면
그것을 이룰 수 있다.

Step by step and the thing is done.

The more we do, the more we can do.

하면 할수록
할 수 있는 것은 더 많아진다.

The more we do, the more we can do.

Comfort

We are new every day.

우리는 매일 새롭다.

We are new every day.

Flowers grow out of dark moments.

꽃은 암흑의 순간에 자라난다.
- 수녀 코리타 켄트 -

Flowers grow out of dark moments.

Everything is gonna be okay.

모든 게 다 괜찮아질 거예요.

Everything is gonna be okay.

Glee! The great storm is over!

기뻐하세요!
힘든 시기가 끝났어요!

Glee! The great storm is over!

The only cure for grief is action.

슬픔의 유일한 치료제는 행동이다.
– 조지 헨리 루이스 –

The only cure for grief is action.

The best is yet to come.

최고의 시기는
아직 오지 않았을 뿐이에요.

The best is yet to come.

Sometimes you just need to breathe.

때때로 당신은
쉬어갈 필요가 있어요.

Sometimes you just need to breathe.

Forget the past and live the present hour.

과거는 잊고 현재의 시간을 살자.

Forget the past and live the present hour.

Hope

Don't lose hope.

희망을 잃지 말자.

Don't lose hope.

Great hopes make great men.

큰 희망이 큰 사람을 만든다.
– 토마스 풀러 –

Great hopes make great men.

No hope, no action.

희망이 없다면 행동도 없다.

No hope, no action.

There is always hope.

항상 희망이 있어요.

There is always hope.

Hope will never be silent.

희망은 침묵하지 않는다.
- 하비 밀크 -

Hope will never be silent.

Pain is real. But so is hope.

고통이 진짜이듯
희망 또한 그러하다.

Pain is real. But so is hope.

While there is life, there is hope.

살아 있는 한 희망은 있다.

While there is life, there is hope.

Hope is the heartbeat of the soul.

희망은 영혼의 심장 박동이다.

Hope is the heartbeat of the soul.

Peace

Inner Peace
내면의 평화

Inner Peace

Let us have peace.
우리에게 평화를 주소서.

Let us have peace.

Love, Peace and Soul
사랑, 평화, 영혼

Love, Peace and Soul

Peace is its own reward.
평화는 그 자체로 보상이다.
- 간디 -

Peace is its own reward.

Peace comes from within.

평화는 내면으로부터 온다.
– 부처 –

Peace comes from within.

You can't find peace by avoiding life.

삶과의 투쟁 없이는 평화도 없다.

You can't find peace by avoiding life.

We won't have peace by afterthought.

나중에 생각해서는 평화를
얻을 수 없을 것이다.
– 노먼 커즌스 –

We won't have peace by afterthought.

Nobody can bring you peace but yourself.

자신 말고는 평화를 가져다줄
사람이 없다.

Nobody can bring you peace but yourself.

Twenty years from now you will be more
disappointed by the things that you didn't
do than by the ones you did do, so throw off
the bowlines, sail away from safe harbor,
catch the trade winds in your sails.
Explore, Dream, Discover.

- Mark Twain

지금으로부터 20년 후 당신은 당신이 한 일들보다는

하지 않은 일들에 더 좌절하게 될 것이다.

그러니 돛을 올리고 지금 당장 당신의 안전한 항구로부터 떠나라.

항해를 하며 바람을 만끽하라.

탐험하라, 꿈을 꾸라, 발견하라.

- 마크 트웨인 -